# STONES
## and
# "STUFF"

**Gareth Stevens Publishing**
A WORLD ALMANAC EDUCATION GROUP COMPANY

**Please visit our web site at: www.garethstevens.com**
**For a free color catalog describing Gareth Stevens Publishing's**
**list of high-quality books and multimedia programs,**
**call 1-800-542-2595 (USA) or 1-800-387-3178 (Canada).**
**Gareth Stevens Publishing's fax: (414) 332-3567.**

**Library of Congress Cataloging-in-Publication Data**

Stones and "stuff."
        p. cm. — (Let's create!)
   Includes bibliographical references.
   Summary: Provides step-by-step instructions for making crafts
using stones, gravel, sand, and other objects, found either in nature
or around the house.
   ISBN 0-8368-4019-4 (lib. bdg.)
   1. Rock craft—Juvenile literature. 2. Shellcraft—Juvenile literature.
3. Handicraft—Juvenile literature. [1. Rock craft. 2. Shellcraft.
3. Nature craft. 4. Handicraft.] I. Title. II. Series.
TT293.P5313 2004
745.5—dc22                       2003057359

This North American edition first published in 2004 by
**Gareth Stevens Publishing**
A World Almanac Education Group Company
330 West Olive Street, Suite 100
Milwaukee, WI 53212 USA

First published as *¡Vamos a crear! Piedras y objetos* with an original copyright © 2001
by Parramón Ediciones, S.A., – World Rights, text and illustrations by Parramón's
Editorial Team. This U.S. edition copyright © 2004 by Gareth Stevens, Inc.
Additional end matter copyright © 2004 by Gareth Stevens, Inc.

English Translation: Colleen Coffey
Gareth Stevens Series Editor: Dorothy L. Gibbs
Gareth Stevens Designer: Katherine A. Goedheer

Printed in Spain

1 2 3 4 5 6 7 8 9 08 07 06 05 04

# Table of Contents

# Introduction

Large and small stones, seashells, sponges, sand, buttons, beads, and balloons are just a few of the items on an almost endless list of objects we can use to create original crafts. Nature provides some of these objects, such as sand, stones, and seashells. Other objects, such as sponges, buttons, and beads, are easy-to-find household items.

Making projects with stones and "stuff" can be both challenging and fun, and your imagination will play an important role. The challenge is looking at stones and other objects and discovering what their shapes remind you of. The fun is developing your ideas into original works of art.

This book will give you a good start on creating crafts from objects. String buttons to make a Wiggly Worm. Turn seashells into Seaside Fashions. Use a balloon for the face of a Blue-haired Belle or paint a few flat rocks and bring The Stone Family to life. Try the projects in this book for practice, then let your imagination take over.

The materials you will need to make the twelve projects on the following pages are easy to find. Just look around you. The only other supplies you will need are scissors, glue, tape, paints, colored pencils, and a few other items commonly used at home or at school.

Watch for special instructions at the end of each project to try other great ideas. Sometimes, making just one small change creates a very different result.

**Original crafts are child's play with stones and "stuff" — so start today!**

# Bath-Sponge Bow Tie

**You might say that this bow tie is "wash-or-wear." It is made out of a colorful bath sponge!**

**You will need:**

- scissors
- cardboard toilet paper tube
- ruler
- pencil
- fuchsia and green poster board
- glue stick
- black elastic string
- large, green, rectangular bath sponge

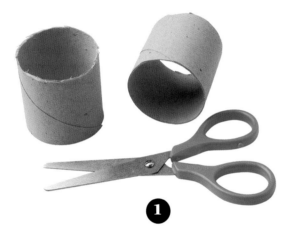

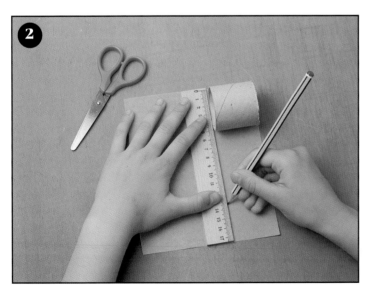

1. Cut a cardboard toilet paper tube in half. Use one half for this project and save the other half for another project.

2. Measure and cut a strip of fuchsia poster board that is the same width as the half toilet paper tube and is just long enough to fit around the tube.

3. Wrap the fuchsia strip around the half toilet paper tube, using a glue stick to attach it.

4. Cut four thin strips of green poster board. Glue them around the fuchsia-covered toilet paper tube, leaving an equal amount of space between each strip.

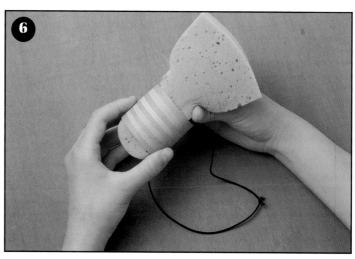

**5** Cut a piece of black elastic string long enough to fit around your head. Thread the elastic string through the toilet paper tube, then tie the ends together in a knot.

**6** Push a large bath sponge into the tube until the tube is around the middle of the sponge.

**Did you ever imagine that a bath sponge could make such nifty neckwear?**

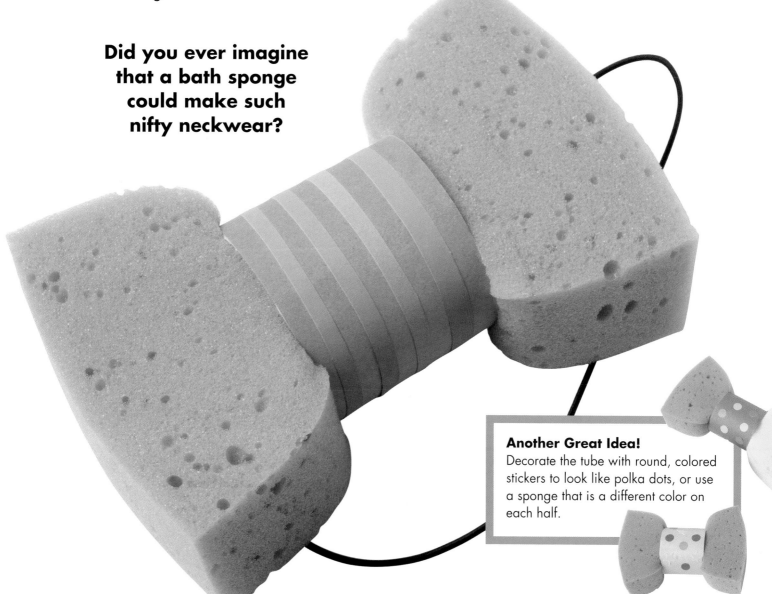

**Another Great Idea!**
Decorate the tube with round, colored stickers to look like polka dots, or use a sponge that is a different color on each half.

7

# The Stone Family

Four flat rocks come to life when you make this friendly family. Dress each family member in brightly colored clothes — then give them names!

**You will need:**
- four round, flat rocks
- different colors of paint
- paintbrush
- white poster board
- pencil
- colored pencils
- scissors
- clear tape

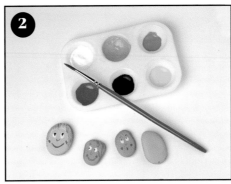

1 Find two small flat rocks and two flat rocks that are a little larger. Paint each rock pink or tan.

2 After the pink paint dries, paint a mouth, a nose, and eyes on each rock to make a face. Also paint on some hair.

3 Place the painted rocks on a piece of white poster board. Using the rocks as heads for a father, a mother, and two children, draw a body with clothing for each family member, making each body the right size for that person.

4 Color the clothing with colored pencils, then cut out each body.

5 Use clear tape to attach a body to the back of each flat rock.

**Meet the Stone family! Don't they look happy to be "alive"?**

**Another Great Idea!**
Create grandparents, aunts, uncles, cousins, and babies for the Stone family. You could even create a pet, such as a dog, a cat, or a pony.

# Bead Baubles

**By combining beads of different shapes, sizes, and colors, you can make dazzling pieces of jewelry. Start with this easy-to-bead necklace and bracelet.**

**You will need:**
- scissors
- thin, green and light brown string
- round, square, and tube-shaped colored beads
- black elastic string

1 To make a necklace, cut two long pieces of thin string, one green and the other light brown. Thread both pieces of string through a yellow tube-shaped bead so that the bead is centered on the strings. Then, thread five round beads on each side of the tube-shaped bead in the following order: green, yellow, white, yellow, green. Tie a knot in the strings behind the last bead on each side.

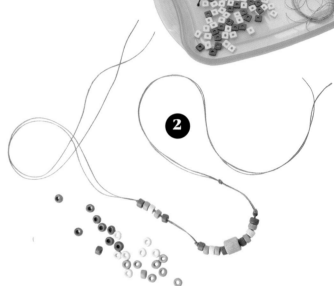

2 Leave a space, then tie another knot in the strings on each side of the center beads. Repeat the sequence of round beads in step 1 on each side of the string.

3 Repeat step 2 several times on each side. Finally, tie the two ends of the green and light brown strings together in a knot.

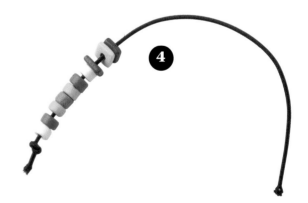

4 To make a bracelet, cut a piece of black elastic string long enough to fit around your wrist. Tie a knot at one end of the string, then thread round and square colored beads onto the string in the order shown in the photograph.

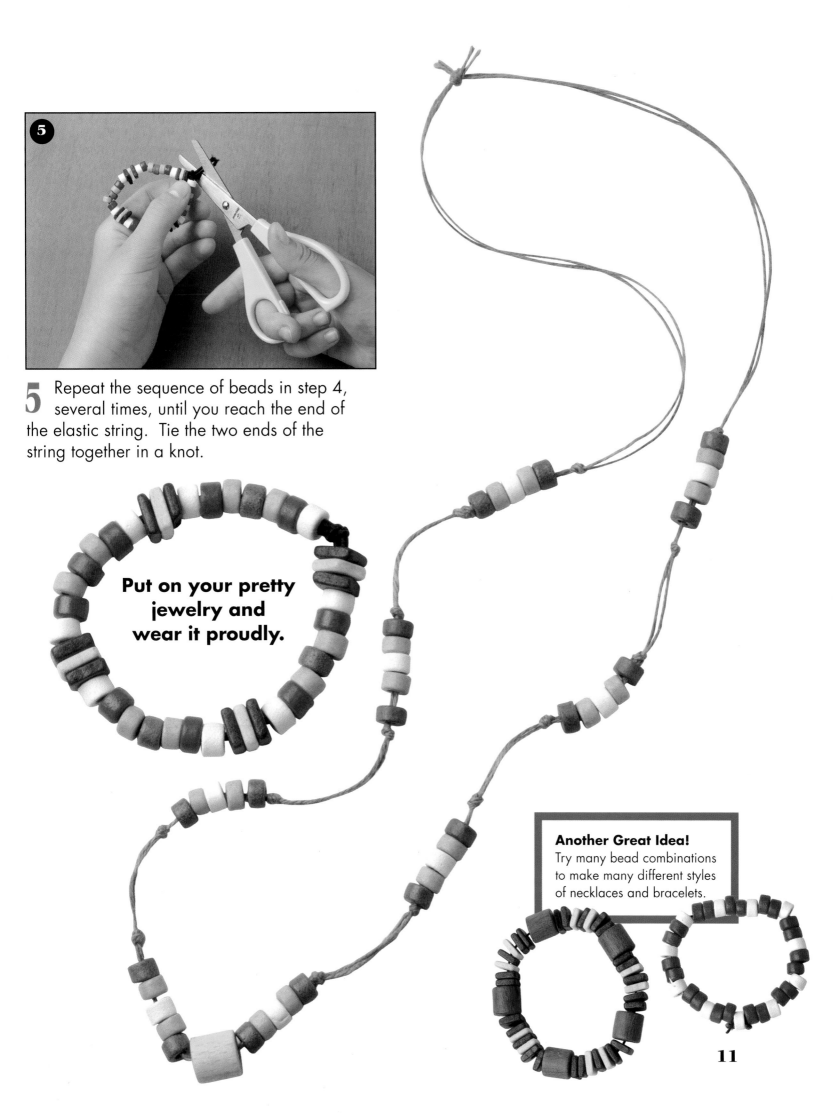

**5** Repeat the sequence of beads in step 4, several times, until you reach the end of the elastic string. Tie the two ends of the string together in a knot.

**Put on your pretty jewelry and wear it proudly.**

**Another Great Idea!**
Try many bead combinations to make many different styles of necklaces and bracelets.

# Blue-Haired Belle

**This fashionable female begins with a balloon.  Her spiky blue hair is a cellophane type of raffia.  Her face and makeup are yours to design.**

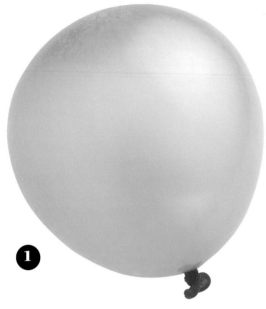

1 Blow up a pink balloon and tie a knot in the neck to hold in the air.

2 Cut blue cellophane raffia into about twenty long strips.

### You will need:
- pink balloon
- scissors
- blue cellophane raffia
- blue tape
- white, green, and red round stickers in different sizes
- large red triangle-shaped stickers
- black marker

3 Attach the strips of raffia to the top of the balloon with blue tape.

4 Cut the raffia any way you want to design a hairdo.

12

**5** To make eyes, stick two white round stickers on the top half of the balloon and two, smaller, green round stickers on top of the white ones. Use a red round sticker for a nose and a red triangle-shaped sticker for a mouth.

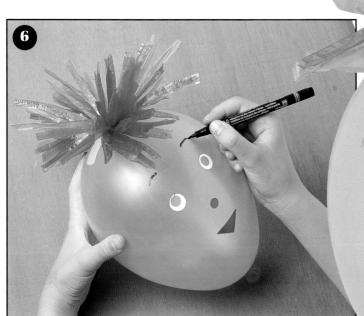

**6** Draw eyebrows on the face with a black marker.

**Another Great Idea!**
Start with an orange balloon and bright red raffia. Draw the eyes, nose, and mouth of a clown on white paper. Paint them or color them with crayons, cut them out, and glue them onto the balloon. Now you have a red-haired circus clown!

**With a smidgen of imagination, you can make original balloon heads of all kinds.**

13

# Beach in a Box

Let nature help you bring a sunny seashore indoors. Sand and stones, which are both natural materials, make this beachscape look real.

## You will need:

- scissors
- large, rectangular cardboard box
- glue stick
- blue, yellow, white, orange, and fuschia paper
- blue and white paints
- paintbrush
- sponge
- fine sand
- liquid school glue
- gray stones
- black marker
- colored pencils
- three small corks
- green tissue paper
- brown thumbtack
- red round stickers
- small colored stones

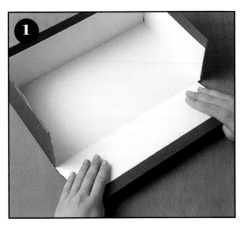

**1** Cut down the corners at each end of one long side of a rectangular cardboard box. Bend that side down so it lays flat and is even with the bottom of the box.

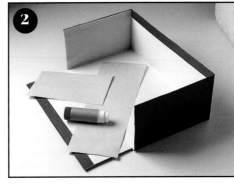

**2** Use a glue stick to attach blue paper to the inside surfaces of the remaining three sides of the box, making blue sky for your beach scene.

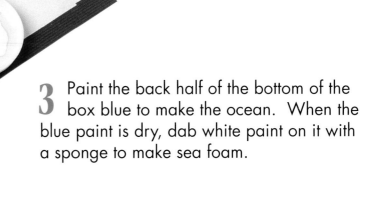

**3** Paint the back half of the bottom of the box blue to make the ocean. When the blue paint is dry, dab white paint on it with a sponge to make sea foam.

14

**4** Use a glue stick to coat the unpainted part of the bottom of the box with glue. Spread sand over the glue, covering the entire surface. Shake the box so the sand that is not glued down will fall off.

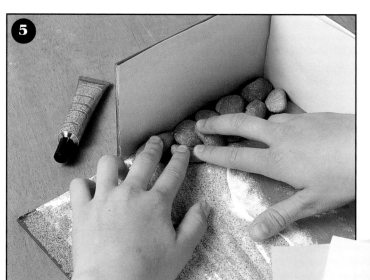

**5** Use liquid school glue to attach gray stones along the side edges of the sand beach.

**6** With a black marker, draw a sun and sun rays on yellow paper and cut them out. Draw a smiling face on the sun with colored pencils. Then, draw two flying birds on white paper and cut them out.

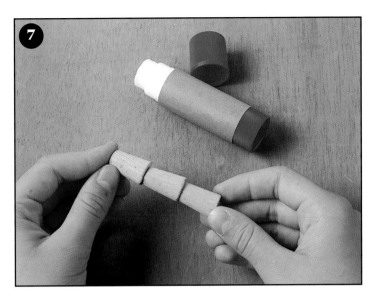

**7** Glue together three small corks to make the trunk of a palm tree.

**8** Cut five short strips of green tissue paper for the leaves of the palm tree. Attach the leaves to the top of the tree's trunk with a brown thumbtack.

**9** Glue the yellow sun and the white birds onto the blue paper that is covering the back of the box. Glue the palm tree to the sand on one side of the beach.

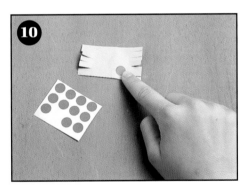

**10** To make a small beach towel, cut a rectangle out of orange paper and cut little slits along each short end to make fringes. Decorate the towel with red round stickers.

**11** Place the towel on the sand under the palm tree and scatter small colored stones across the sand beach.

**12** Fold fuchsia paper into the shape of a boat and place the boat in the ocean.

**On a cold day, just look at your beautiful beach scene and imagine that you are someplace very warm!**

**Another Great Idea!**
Add larger stones, a hammock, a beach umbrella, or anything else that comes to mind, to change your beach scene from time to time.

# Wiggly Worm

**A strip of buttons makes this colorful little worm very flexible. Thin elastic string makes it even more wiggly.**

**You will need:**
- thin black elastic string
- 2- or 4-holed buttons in a variety of bright colors
- orange, red, black, and green paints
- paintbrush
- small paper ball
- yarn needle

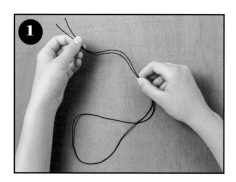

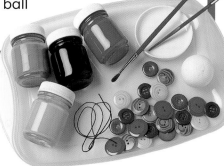

**1** Cut a piece of thin black elastic string so it is about 24 inches (60 centimeters) long, then fold the string in half.

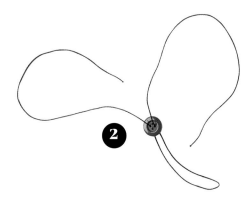

**2** Thread a colored button onto the string by putting each end of the elastic string, separately, through two holes in the button.

**3** Repeat step 2, adding more colored buttons in any order you wish.

**4** Paint a paper ball orange.

**5** When the orange paint is dry, paint on a red mouth, nose, and cheeks, two black eyes, and green hair.

**18**

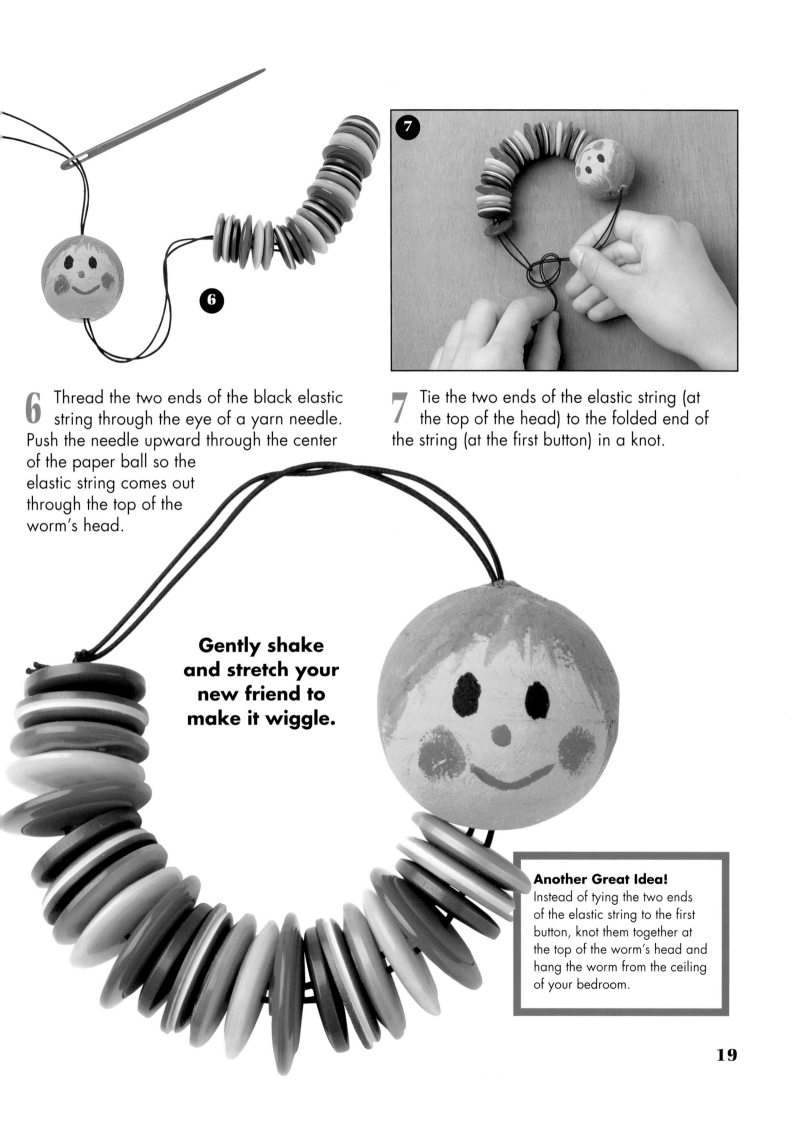

**6** Thread the two ends of the black elastic string through the eye of a yarn needle. Push the needle upward through the center of the paper ball so the elastic string comes out through the top of the worm's head.

**7** Tie the two ends of the elastic string (at the top of the head) to the folded end of the string (at the first button) in a knot.

**Gently shake and stretch your new friend to make it wiggle.**

**Another Great Idea!**
Instead of tying the two ends of the elastic string to the first button, knot them together at the top of the worm's head and hang the worm from the ceiling of your bedroom.

**19**

# Seaside Fashions

**A scallop shell is the perfect shape for making a skirt or the bottom of a dress.  Watch how quickly and cleverly you can create a whole seashell wardrobe.**

1 Paint several medium-sized scallop shells any colors you wish.

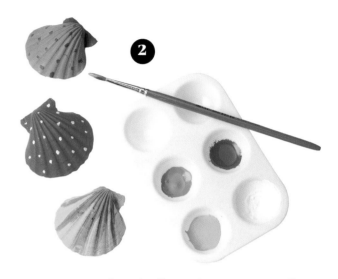

2 Decorate the shells with stripes, polka dots, and other designs, painted in contrasting colors.

## You will need:
- different colors of paint
- paintbrush
- scallop shells
- black marker
- white cardboard
- colored pencils
- scissors
- self-adhesive Velcro

3 Draw a picture of a girl on white cardboard and color the picture with colored pencils.

4 Cut pieces of self-adhesive Velcro. Stick one side of the Velcro to the drawing, at the girl's waist.  Stick the other side of the Velcro to the hinge edge on the inside of each decorated shell.

**5** Attach a shell "skirt" to the drawing by sticking the Velcro pieces together.

**With several shell fashions, you can change the girl's clothes whenever you want!**

**Another Great Idea!**
Put a piece of self-adhesive Velcro at the top of the girl's head on your drawing, then use the decorated shells as hair or hats.

21

# Mouse Maze

**Help a mouse find its way to the cheese! This entertaining maze is easy to make. The "mouse" is actually a marble. The maze is just a plastic box and a few sheets of colored foam paper.**

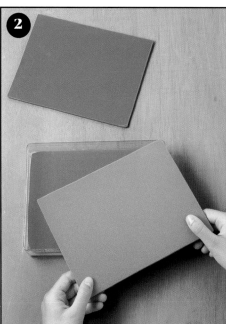

1 Cut four sheets of foam paper, two blue and two red, to fit in the bottom of a clear plastic box.

2 Alternating colors (red, blue, red), put three of the sheets of foam paper in the bottom of the box.

3 Cut the third sheet of red foam paper into strips that are the same width but are different lengths.

4 Cut two rectangles out of a piece of white poster board. Use black marker to draw a mouse on one of the rectangles and a wedge of cheese on the other. Color the mouse and the cheese drawings with colored pencils.

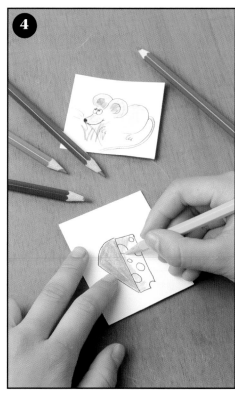

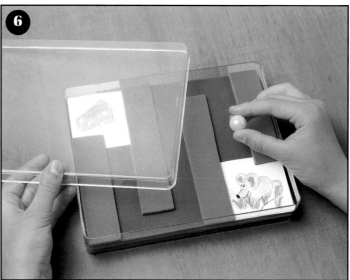

**5** Place the drawings in two opposite corners on the remaining sheet of blue foam paper, using glue stick to attach them. Glue the red foam-paper strips onto the blue foam paper in an arrangement that forms a maze.

**6** Place the maze and a marble inside the box, then cover the box with its clear plastic lid.

**Tip, tilt, and turn the box to roll the "mouse" through the maze until it reaches the cheese.**

**Another Great Idea!**
Make different drawings, such as a rabbit and a carrot, or make your maze more difficult by creating dead ends with the foam-paper strips.

# Rainbow in a Jar

A clever crafter can find many uses for sand and colored chalk. But did you ever think of combining them to create a beautiful rainbow? Here's one easy way to do it!

**1** Fill one-third of a glass jar with sand.

**2** Break red, green, yellow, blue, and violet colored chalk into small pieces. Put each color of chalk into a separate plastic bag.

## You will need:

- glass jar with a lid
- fine sand
- red, green, yellow, blue, and violet colored chalk
- 5 plastic bags
- large stone
- wooden pestle
- scissors
- yellow crepe paper
- black elastic string

**3** Carefully press down on the chalk in each bag with a large stone to smash the chalk into powder. Be careful that you do not break the bag so the powder does not seep out.

**4** Pour red chalk powder on top of the sand in the glass jar. Press the red powder down as much as you can with a wooden pestle.

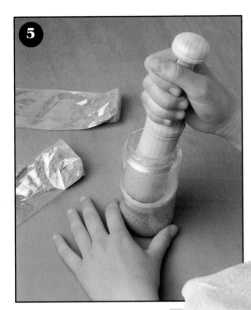

**5** Repeat step 4 with the other four colors of chalk powder, pressing down each layer with the wooden pestle before you add the next color.

**6** Fill the rest of the jar with sand, then put on the lid.

**Look! You have captured a rainbow.**

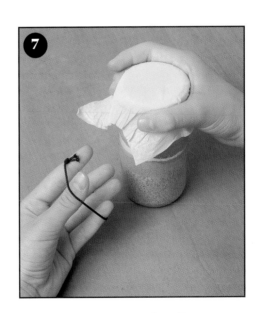

**7** Cut a square of yellow crepe paper and spread it over the lid of the jar. Tie black elastic string around the crepe paper to hold it in place.

**Another Great Idea!**
Use jars of different shapes to make even more decorative rainbows, or use two large jars to make rainbow bookends.

# Perky Paperweight

**Keep that stack of papers neat and tidy — and decorate your desk at the same time — with this bright-eyed flower paperweight.**

1 Paint all sides of a large, round, flat stone green.

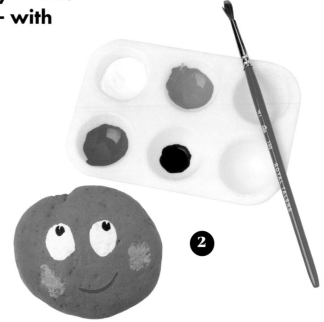

2 When the green paint is dry, paint white and black eyes and a red mouth and cheeks on one side of the stone.

## You will need:
- green, white, black, and red paints
- paintbrushes
- large, round, flat stone
- orange poster board
- black marker
- scissors
- liquid school glue

3 Place the stone on a piece of orange poster board. With a black marker, draw the petals of a flower around the stone.

26

4 Cut the flower figure out of the poster board.

5 Attach the painted stone to the center of the flower with liquid school glue.

**This cheerful-looking paperweight can make even homework seem like fun.**

**Another Great Idea!**
Use a flat, oval-shaped stone to make a colorful tropical fish paperweight.

# Jingle-Bell Chime

**Bells and beads will make beautiful music together when you create this wind chime.**

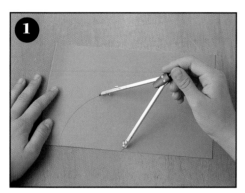

**1** Using a compass, draw a semicircle with a radius of 3 inches (8 centimeters) on a piece of blue poster board.

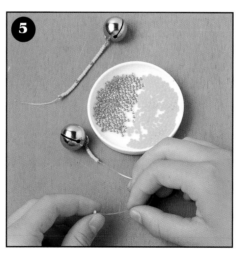

**2** Cut out the semicircle and tape the straight sides of it together, forming the shape of a cone.

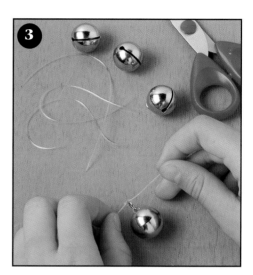

**3** Cut four pieces of clear plastic thread, making all of the pieces the same length. Tie a jingle bell to the end of each piece of thread.

**4** On two of the pieces of plastic thread, string ten blue beads, then two yellow beads, above the jingle bell. Repeat this step three times, ending with ten blue beads.

**You will need:**
- compass
- blue poster board
- scissors
- clear tape
- clear plastic thread
- 4 jingle bells
- blue and yellow beads
- yellow thread

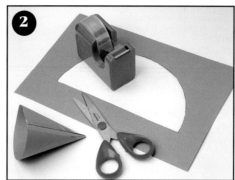

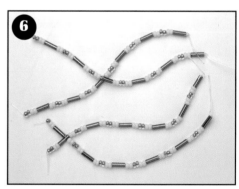

**5** On the other two pieces of plastic thread, string two blue beads, then ten yellow. Repeat this step three times, ending with two blue beads.

**6** Cut four more pieces of plastic thread and tie a knot at one end of each piece. String sets of two blue, two yellow, and one blue tube-shaped bead on each piece of thread until the thread is filled with beads.

**7** Tape the eight strands of beads to the inside of the cone, alternating strands with jingle bells and strands without jingle bells.

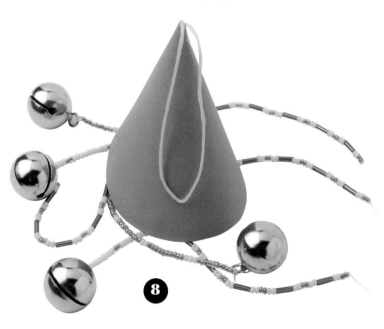

**8** Tape a loop of yellow thread to the tip of the cone so you will be able to hang your wind chime.

**Another Great Idea!**
Decorate the outside of the cone with two strings of colored beads.

**Hang your jingle-bell chime on the back of a door so it will ring each time the door opens or closes.**

# Clown Surprise

**When your friends open this decorated glass jar, they will never expect the springy surprise you put inside. Grab a sponge and have some fun!**

1 Coat the inside of a glass jar with glue and sprinkle green glitter over the glue until the inside of the jar is covered.

2 Decorate the outside of the jar with small yellow star stickers. Put a larger star sticker in the center of the lid.

3 On white poster board, trace around the lid of the jar with a black marker. This circle shows you the size to make the clown's face.

4 With colored pencils, draw the face of a clown inside the circle. Then cut the clown's face out of the circle.

**5** Cut a narrow strip off of a pink bath sponge. The strip must be able to fit inside the jar.

**6** Glue the clown's face to one end of the sponge strip.

**7** Put the sponge strip inside the jar with the clown's face at the top. Then put the lid on the jar.

## When you uncover the jar, watch out!

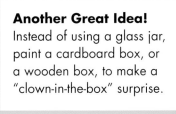

**Another Great Idea!**
Instead of using a glass jar, paint a cardboard box, or a wooden box, to make a "clown-in-the-box" surprise.

# Glossary

**baubles:** showy ornaments or trinkets

**belle:** a pretty young woman or little girl

**cellophane:** strong, see-through paper with a shiny, filmlike surface

**contrasting:** looking noticeably different

**fuschia:** a deep, bright pink color named for the blossom of the fuschia plant

**hinge:** a joint that connects two parts of a thing, allowing movement back and forth

**pestle:** a kitchen tool with a ball-shaped end that is used to crush dry solids

**raffia:** a strawlike type of ribbon

**scallop:** a type of shellfish, belonging to the clam family, with a two-part shell that opens and closes

**sequence:** the order or arrangement of one thing following another

**smidgen:** small amount

**Velcro:** the trademark name for a type of fastener that has tiny nylon hooks on one side and soft nylon loops on the other side

**wedge: (n)** a shape with one wide end that slopes to a thin edge at the other end

# More Books to Read

*Extraordinary Projects from Ordinary Objects #1. Look, Learn & Do* (series). Mark Icanberry (Look, Learn, and Do)

*Fun Factory: Games and Toys from Household Junk.* Lyndsay Milne (Reader's Digest)

*Look What I Did with a Shell! NatureCraft* (series). Morteza E. Sohi (Walker & Co.)

*Odds 'n' Ends Art. Handy Crafts* (series). Gillian Souter (Gareth Stevens)

*Painting on Rocks for Kids.* Lin Wellford (North Light Books)

# Web Sites

*Making Friends: Beaded Decorations.* www.makingfriends.com/ponybead/decorations.htm

*Pebble and Rock Crafts.* www.enchantedlearning.com/crafts/pebbles/